Shift Your Trajectory

15 Habits To

Financially Thrive

Destiny S. Harris

...

Copyright © 2023 Destiny S. Harris.

All rights reserved. No part of this publication may be reproduced without prior written permission from the author, except in the case of quotations.

I don't care if you share my work. Just be sure to create work of your own. You have infinite creative ability; use it.

Front cover image by Destiny S. Harris.

Book design by Destiny S. Harris.

First printing edition 2023.

www.destinyh.com

1st Free Gift!

Giving Rocks.

I give away free books daily.

Get your free books today.

Here's how

Step 1: Visit amazon.com/author/destinyharris

Step 2: Filter books by "Price: Low to High"

Step 3: Download available free books

. . .

Table of Contents

. . .

. . .

Disclaimer

This book is for informational purposes only. It should not be considered Financial or Legal Advice. Not all information will be accurate. Consult a financial professional before making any significant financial decisions.

. . .

A Thought

Do you want to level up financially?

Implement the following 15 habits and notice a change in your finances instantly. Some things just work; it's that simple.

. . .

15 Habits

Habit 1

1. Invest 15–25% or more of your income

That's right. Not 10% of your income. 15–25%+ of your income. I always believe 25% is a better way to go, but that's a personal preference. Your savings rate will grow as you acquire more income, and this will help you establish five things:

- Financial security

- Financial freedom

- Financial peace

- Financial discipline

- Financial elevation.

Most people save nothing **or** save around 10% of their income. Those who save around 10% of their income often still end up broke when retirement comes around. How does that work?

Because 10% of an average income will help you end up with average savings. Take the more aggressive approach when it comes to saving, and you'll end up a little bit happier in the end.

. . .

Habit 2

2. Maintain a 2-year emergency fund

There is a minimum of 12 reasons to have a stocked and stacked 2-year emergency fund:

1: Peace of mind

2: Financial freedom

3: Mitigate job dependency

4: Be prepared for most emergencies

5: Have liquid assets that are easily accessible

6: Cover any living expenses for two years

7: Recession-proof your finances

8: Focus on investing

9: Never be broke

10: A 3-6 month emergency fund goes by quickly

11: Have enough resources to more than scrape

by

12: Take time off

. . .

Habit 3

3. Live below your means

This **is** the most salient financial habit to implement. If you implement this one habit, you guarantee yourself almost 99% success financially.

When you live below your means, you will always have money in the bank. You will remain out of debt and avoid living paycheck to paycheck.

. . .

Habit 4

4. Live debt-free

Here are the most common types of debt [see immediately below]. You probably have at least one or more of these types of debts, or you've probably *had* one or more of these types of debts at some point. The majority **maintains** debt instead of eradicating debt.

- Credit card debt

- Student loans

- Car loans

- Personal loans

- Medical bills

- Property loans

You can do the opposite of the majority and live **without** debt; it's an unusual way to live but also an exhilarating and liberating manner of living. Owe no one anything.

Proverbs 6:1–7 *says, "If you've signed surety, my son, do this. Give no sleep to your eyelids, no slumber to your eyes, and deliver yourself like a gazelle from the hand of the hunter [..]." A powerful nugget of wisdom that we should implement.*

...

Habit 5

5. Live below your means

Avoid lifestyle creep like the plague. Most people don't live below their means because doing the opposite is ingrained.

Consumerism is an unspoken and widespread addiction.

We are fed the following messages:

- We got to live the fabulous social media-worthy type lifestyle.

- We got to have the latest iPhone or iPad.

- We got to have a life *worth* imitating.

- We got to have the *things* we are taught to obtain to live a "fulfilling" life.

"So, concerning the things we pursue and for which we vigorously exert ourselves, we owe this consideration — either there is nothing useful in them, or most aren't useful. Some of them are superfluous, while others aren't worth that much.

But we don't discern this and see them as free when they cost us dearly." — The Daily Stoic p 75

. . .

Habit 6

6. Enable your money to work for you through <u>investing</u>.

<u>Investing</u> allows you to utilize compound interest to your advantage, saving far more money than you could if you saved in a low-interest-rate savings account. The interest rates you receive from investing most often far outweigh any money you earn in a savings account.

<u>Investing</u> is both a critical and powerful tool. You don't have to have a degree in finance or economics to understand this. You don't have to be a financial genius to invest your money. All

you need to do is find a solid, reputable financial

firm or bank, or even start using your employer's

401k option (if you are working or have this

benefit at your job), and start investing your

money today.

. . .

Habit 7

7. Consistently implement viable ideas to increase your income.

Something most people don't do is write down ideas when they come to mind. And since most people don't write down their goals, most do not write down 20 ideas — to help them reach their goals.

Earl Nightingale said it best, "Men simply don't think." Instead, they spend most of their time watching the tube and wake up one day and realize they're 65, and they've not tapped into their infinite potential by an inch.

Spend 10–15 minutes each day writing ideas to help you reach your goals faster. Some ideas will be mediocre, some will be great, and some will be legendary. Don't underestimate the power of an idea and writing things down.

Never cease increasing your income.

. . .

Habit 8

8. <u>Increase your income sources</u> — especially passive income.

Depending upon one basket of income is like betting your life savings on **one** horse.

Maintaining multiple sources of income is one key to establishing a solid financial foundation (as far as income goes). None of us can ever predict the future 100%, so why do so many of us live as if we can?

What are your talents? What are you good at? What are you interested in? Be creative and find ways to capitalize on your talents and interests while also working your primary job(s). I suggest always having at least 3–10 different sources of income; if you find this to be too much to do, aim for a minimum of 2 different sources of income.

I guarantee that having multiple sources of income will:

1. Relieve financial pressure

2. Eradicate dependence on any one source of income or company

3. Give you more freedom

Passive income streams (e.g., royalties from books, music, and other intellectual property and real estate) are best because they generate money without you needing to invest time and effort consistently. Another popular option is to have a full-time gig and a part-time gig. **Again, never depend on one source of income.**

. . .

Habit 9

9. <u>Educate</u> yourself on everything finance to inspire new ways of thinking.

If you're not learning, you're not growing.

Ignorance is not bliss. <u>Read as if your life depended on it</u>. The more you educate yourself, the better the life you'll experience.

Utilized knowledge is power.

. . .

Habit 10

10. Surround yourself with wealthy individuals.

The majority doesn't have $500 in their bank account to cover an emergency expense, which means the majority is one step away from being broke or already broke. I'm not even taking into consideration the fact that most people are also in debt. Establish new relationships with individuals that can challenge your level of thinking and elevate your financial status.

. . .

Habit 11

11. Engage in <u>entrepreneurship</u>, and work for yourself.

The best kind of job is where you're the boss, and you determine your earnings, schedule, benefits, income, and workload. Entrepreneurship gives you back the power to create your reality and set the tone for your financial future. At least one of your income sources should be from entrepreneurship.

. . .

Habit 12

12. Embrace <u>minimalism</u>.

Implementing the practice of minimalism will ensure you don't buy things without a definite and meaningful reason.

I wrote an article called "<u>Desires Make You A Servant</u>" that belabors the idea:

If you want nothing, you have everything. You're in control, and no one has leverage over you. Not businesses, advertisements, societal "norms," people, or desires.

How often do we witness people buy the new car, only to watch them constantly work to pay for it?

They **have** to **keep** working, and if they don't, their car will be repossessed (not to mention their credit will get f*cked up).

Minimalism helps you avoid buying into the idea that you need to buy all the time, every day, and the things you don't need.

"[...] in a society of ever-bigger houses and ever more possessions: [..] there's a hidden cost to all of that accumulating." — The Daily Stoic p 75

Our health (financial, mental, physical, emotional, and spiritual) and our peace are the hidden costs.

Habit 13

13. Study the top 1% of the wealthiest 1%; pick their brains.

Read articles and books, attend conferences, and learn from the top 1%. Not to attain the money they acquired but to learn what works and doesn't work for business, finance, investing, habits, productivity, and entrepreneurship.

. . .

Habit 14

14. <u>Think</u> thoughts focusing on wealth, prosperity, and abundance.

Something you won't often hear from a wealthy person with a wealthy mentality is: "I'm broke." Wealthy people focus on prosperity, attracting more wealth, and think in terms of abundance.

. . .

Habit 15

15. <u>Increase</u> your self-worth.

People with high self-worth do not settle for less in life. They believe they are worthy of financial independence. They negotiate higher pay, income, and salaries. They don't allow life to hand them whatever; they demand from life what they desire and create opportunities to succeed.

. . .

Thank You For Reading

Thank you for reading this book.

Stay blessed, lucky, favored, aware, joyous, and committed to bettering yourself.

. . .

The End.

. . .

. . .

About Destiny S. Harris

Destiny S. Harris' goal is to positively inspire, cultivate, elevate, and educate the minds of individuals across the globe through her writing.

Creating (whether books, courses, articles, poetry, or music) has always been Destiny's thing, not to mention health & fitness and all things entrepreneurial. Destiny published her first book, "Beauty Secrets for Girls," at age 11 and her second book, "Don't Wait Until It's Too Late," at age 12.

Destiny obtained three degrees in Psychology, Political Science, & Cultural Studies. She also started her own music teaching business at the age of 14, which she led for over ten years. In addition, she has been teaching academic, career, and personal development topics to thousands of students and readers since 2004.

Outside of writing, Destiny loves and enjoys a few other things: reading, weightlifting, traveling, football, dogs, food, classic movies, mountain and ocean views, sleeping, plants, and nature.

Check out her work, leave a review, share your thoughts with your friends and family, and be a part of a movement: helping people learn and grow through means of self-education (books).

<u>**Complete the Steps To Get Free eBooks:**</u>

Step 1: Go to amazon.com/author/destinyharris

Step 2: Filter books by "Price: Low to High"

Step 3: Download available free books

. . .

Connect W/ Destiny S. Harris

Please reach out and stay in touch. Destiny S. Harris enjoys chatting with readers.

Start a conversation today @ destinyh.com

. . .

Free Gifts!

Access courses & free eBooks at the link below:

destinyh.com

. . .

www.ingramcontent.com/pod-product-compliance
Lightning Source LLC
Chambersburg PA
CBHW060840260726
48661CB00002B/524